I

I

I

The Original 1841 Essay by
Ralph Waldo Emerson

Plus Twelve New Essays by
Jessica Helfand

SELF RELI ANC E

THE VALUE OF +
BARRIERS TO SELF-RELIANCE

14

+ **Twelve Essays** by **Jessica Helfand**

Originally published on Design Observer
during the COVID-19 pandemic, 2020

by Ralph Waldo Emerson

2 3

I CAN BE

intoxicated

with beauty

LOSE MY
SADNESS

On learning.

I learned how to be alone the hard way.

My mother died when I was still young and my own children were small. Within a decade, I would also lose my husband. Personal loss, always irrevocable, became an all-out war, an assault on the psyche, and a blow (many blows, actually) to the heart.

I was suffering, but I was impatient. I'd been abandoned, and I felt ashamed. I felt sorry for myself, angry at the world, and envious of everyone else who, I was certain, had it way better than I did. Weekends were onerous. Social media was hell. I was mournful of the past, worried for the future, and seemingly incapable of processing any of it.

But when, just a few years after the loss of my children's father, my own father died, everything stopped. I couldn't work or sleep or eat. I cried at the slightest provocation. I canceled my classes, withdrew from everything, and hid from everyone.

This newly minted round of loss led to an unprecedented sense of personal dislocation: without warning, it seemed, I'd lost myself. Which required that I find myself. And which I did, quite simply, by returning to the studio.

In the spring of 2020, as the first waves of the COVID-19 virus surged, I was finishing up an artist's residency in Los Angeles when California issued the nation's first stay-at-home order. Other states would follow, then other countries would follow, and suddenly the world had stopped once again.

This time, I was ready.

Locked down and on my own some three thousand miles from home, I walked the periphery of my studio, in choreographically limited loops, logging upwards of six miles daily. By day, technology offered the illusion of staying connected (to what, I'm not certain), while at night I painted portraits of the newscasters appearing on my TV screen, the only people I was seeing on a regular basis. As the days wore on, I found myself thinking increasingly about isolation and loneliness, about what it meant to secede from structure, to pierce the forcefield of routine. I thought about leaderless teams and rudderless weeks, and about the systems upon which all of us, for so many reasons (and for so long), have come to rely. Some of those systems are conversational: we rely on being in dialogue with others. Some are congregational: we rely on being in the company of others. And some are computational: we rely on a non-human (but non-stop) infrastructure of coordinated technologies that serve as our tireless, if remote, proxies. When quarantine went global, that alt-circuitry kicked into overdrive, social distancing a catalyst to sentient dislocation.

All of which begged the question: when so much of what you've been groomed to rely upon vanishes from view, where do you go?

Enter Emerson.

"To talk of reliance is a poor external way of speaking," he wrote. "Speak rather of that which relies, because it works and is."

This is the essence of Emerson's seminal essay on self-reliance, originally published in 1841 and reproduced here in its entirety (which is to say, unedited). A cursory glance may grate on the sensitive reader. This is, after all, the writing of a supremely confident man, whose language reflects the privilege and purview of a different era. American, Caucasian, schooled in the liturgical (and with a flair for the theatrical), Emerson made his living as a lecturer, and his authoritative tone can read as discomfiting, even didactic.

But a closer read reveals something far more meaningful and relevant. This is a meditation on what it means to be human, to have an imagination, and to use it.

Emerson's writing lacks pretense, yet abounds in spirit. His intellectual reach is capacious, but his emotional truth is unwavering. There is piety and there is poetry, but what resonates most unequivocally here is his plea for individuality—that "iron string"—the sovereignty of selfhood. To read Emerson today is to rethink the flawed calculus that's led you to equate value with consensus, and to imagine instead what it might mean to hear your own voice, to heed your own motives, to hold fast to your own capacity for reason, reflection, and wonder.

Wonder is key. Emerson was, as the late American literary critic Harold Bloom once observed, the dominant sage of the American imagination. Prolific and charismatic, he inspired writers from Emily Dickinson to Walt Whitman, Henry James to Hart Crane. Robert Frost adored him. Robert Penn Warren did not—he called him the devil—and it bears saying that not all of Emerson's ideas were worthy. (He believed, for instance, that Texas should secede from the Union.) He could be kooky, often endearingly so, and had his share of conspiracy theories. Ever the non-conformist, he occasionally viewed history as an impertinence. This is a man who, after all, once referred to himself as a transparent eyeball. Were he to be alive today, noted Bloom, he'd be a performance artist.

Artists, of course, are all too familiar with addressing the sorts of questions best answered by process itself (we sometimes call this thinking through making). But what are the questions, and what is the process? How do you start, and where do you end? The shifting coordinates of a global pandemic unsettle even the most seasoned and skilled among us—and how could they not? Here, Emerson's call to independence is not so much an edict as an invitation: less a reckoning than a beckoning. In the spirit of that invitation, the twelve accompanying essays in this volume address various aspects of creative engagement—writing, drawing,

thinking, making—not intended
as reinterpretations of a canonical
essay, but as reactions to it. Framed
as a way to rethink creative practice,
they consider, both individually and
collectively, how to push that practice
forward, and let it push you right back.

In the end, self-reliance pushes back,
too. Our individual survival requires
nothing less. Good days meet bad
days, aspiration derailed by the pain of
unbidden circumstance. Emerson, for
his part, was no stranger to sorrow.
He lost his first wife to tuberculosis
at the age of twenty, and his first child
to scarlet fever at the age of five—a
scant year after writing this essay.
Did his faith waver, ineffable goodness
overtaken by unspeakable grief?
Perhaps the honesty protected him.
(Perhaps the writing rescued him.)
Or perhaps Emerson simply
understood what so many of us do
not: that life is one infinite loop, one
ever-present Möbius strip of hope
mixed with hurt. Long before a global
pandemic would oblige us to steer

clear of one another, more than a
century before lockdowns interfered
with our best laid plans, Emerson
knew better.

"The days pass over me," he wrote.
"And I am still the same."

Self-reliance is where it all begins,
and ends, and begins once again.
Maybe this is the real infinite loop:
that hard-won human circuitry
that sustains us through so much
ambiguity, uncertainty, and loss.

"Nothing is at last sacred," Emerson
noted, "but the integrity of your own
mind."

Learning to be alone, it turns out,
is the easy part.

Jessica Helfand

A Note on the Text

First published in 1841, "Self-Reliance" is reproduced here in its entirety, retaining the wording, spelling, and stylistic preferences of Ralph Waldo Emerson's original essay.

The first edition of this essay was published in conjunction with three epigraphs, beginning with a Latin phrase that translates to "do not seek outside yourself."

> *Ne te quaesiveris extra*

Following this sentence, Emerson included the epilogue to Beaumont and Fletcher's *Honest Man's Fortune*:

> Man is his own star; and the soul that can
> Render an honest and a perfect man,
> Commands all light, all influence, all fate;
> Nothing to him falls early or too late.
> Our acts our angels are, or good or ill,
> Our fatal shadows that walk by us still.

The epigraphs conclude with a four-line stanza that Emerson wrote himself:

> Cast the bantling on the rocks,
> Suckle him with the she-wolf's teat;
> Wintered with the hawk and fox,
> Power and speed be hands and feet.

While Emerson does not formally do so, scholars conventionally organize "Self-Reliance" into the three sections in this volume.

SELF-RELIANCE

RALPH WALDO EMERSON

✢ BARRIERS TO **THE VALUE OF SELF-RELIANCE**

READ THE OTHER DAY SOME VERSES WRITTEN
by an eminent painter which were original and not conven-
tional. The soul always hears an admonition in such lines,
let the subject be what it may. The sentiment they instil
is of more value than any thought they may contain. To
believe your own thought, to believe that what is true for
you in your private heart is true for all men,—that is genius.
Speak your latent conviction, and it shall be the universal
sense; for the inmost in due time becomes the outmost,—
and our first thought is rendered back to us by the trumpets
of the Last Judgment. Familiar as the voice of the mind is
to each, the highest merit we ascribe to Moses, Plato, and
Milton is, that they set at naught books and traditions, and
spoke not what men but what they thought. A man should
learn to detect and watch that gleam of light which flashes
across his mind from within, more than the lustre of the
firmament of bards and sages. Yet he dismisses without
notice his thought, because it is his. In every work of genius
we recognize our own rejected thoughts: they come back
to us with a certain alienated majesty. Great works of
art have no more affecting lesson for us than this. They
teach us to abide by our spontaneous impression with
good-humored inflexibility then most when the whole cry

We but
half **express**
ourselves,
and are
ashamed
of that
divine idea
which each
of us
represents.

of voices is on the other side. Else, to-morrow a stranger will say with masterly good sense precisely what we have thought and felt all the time, and we shall be forced to take with shame our own opinion from another.

There is a time in every man's education when he arrives at the conviction that envy is ignorance; that imitation is suicide; that he must take himself for better, for worse, as his portion; that though the wide universe is full of good, no kernel of nourishing corn can come to him but through his toil bestowed on that plot of ground which is given to him to till. The power which resides in him is new in nature, and none but he knows what that is which he can do, nor does he know until he has tried. Not for nothing one face, one character, one fact, makes much impression on him, and another none. This sculpture in the memory is not without preestablished harmony. The eye was placed where one ray should fall, that it might testify of that particular ray. We but half express ourselves, and are ashamed of that divine idea which each of us represents. It may be safely trusted as proportionate and of good issues, so it be faithfully imparted, but God will not have his work made manifest by cowards. A man is relieved and gay when he has put his heart into his work and done his best; but what he has said or done otherwise, shall give him no peace. It is a deliverance which does not deliver. In the attempt his genius deserts him; no muse befriends; no invention, no hope.

Trust thyself: every heart vibrates to that iron string. Accept the place the divine providence has found for you, the society of your contemporaries, the connection of events. Great men have always done so, and confided themselves childlike to the genius of their age, betraying their perception that the absolutely trustworthy was seated at their heart, working through their hands, predominating in all their being. And we are now men, and must accept in the highest mind the same transcendent destiny; and not minors and invalids in a protected corner, not cowards fleeing before a revolution, but guides, redeemers, and benefactors, obeying the Almighty effort, and advancing on Chaos and the Dark.

What pretty oracles nature yields us on this text, in the face and behaviour of children, babes, and even brutes! That divided and rebel mind, that distrust of a sentiment because our arithmetic has computed the strength and means opposed to our purpose, these

Long before the lure of mobile technology would make social media a theater all its own, the psychologist Erving Goffman wrote about dramaturgical loyalty, which is what happens when you feel obligated to keep up appearances, playing the part you're meant to play, even if it's disingenuous. (The question of loyalty is a curious one. To whom are you loyal if not yourself?)

On **gravity**
68

These are the

have not. Their mind being whole, their eye is as yet unconquered, and when we look in their faces, we are disconcerted. Infancy conforms to nobody: all conform to it, so that one babe commonly makes four or five out of the adults who prattle and play to it. So God has armed youth and puberty and manhood no less with its own piquancy and charm, and made it enviable and gracious and its claims not to be put by, if it will stand by itself. Do not think the youth has no force, because he cannot speak to you and me. Hark! in the next room his voice is sufficiently clear and emphatic. It seems he knows how to speak to his contemporaries. Bashful or bold, then, he will know how to make us seniors very unnecessary.

The nonchalance of boys who are sure of a dinner, and would disdain as much as a lord to do or say aught to conciliate one, is the healthy attitude of human nature. A boy is in the parlour what the pit is in the playhouse; independent, irresponsible, looking out from his corner on such people and facts as pass by, he tries and sentences

voices

WHICH WE HEAR IN SOLITUDE

them on their merits, in the swift, summary way of boys, as good, bad, interesting, silly, eloquent, troublesome. He cumbers himself never about consequences, about interests: he gives an independent, genuine verdict. You must court him: he does not court you. But the man is, as it were, clapped into jail by his consciousness. As soon as he has once acted or spoken with eclat, he is a committed person, watched by the sympathy or the hatred of hundreds, whose affections must now enter into his account. There is no Lethe for this. Ah, that he could pass again into his neutrality! Who can thus avoid all pledges, and having observed, observe again from the same unaffected, unbiased, unbribable, unaffrighted innocence, must always be formidable. He would utter opinions on all passing affairs, which being seen to be not private, but necessary, would sink like darts into the ear of men, and put them in fear.

These are the voices which we hear in solitude, but they grow faint and inaudible as we enter into the world. Society everywhere is in conspiracy against the manhood of every one of its members. Society is a joint-stock company, in which the members agree, for the better securing of his bread to each shareholder, to surrender the liberty and culture of the eater. The virtue in most request is conformity. Self-reliance is its aversion. It loves not realities and creators, but names and customs.

Whoso would be a man must be a nonconformist. He who would gather immortal palms must not be hindered by the name of goodness, but must explore if it be goodness. Nothing is at last sacred but the integrity of your own mind. Absolve you to yourself, and you shall have the suffrage of the world. I remember an answer which when quite young I was prompted to make to a valued adviser, who was wont to importune me with the dear old doctrines of the church. On my saying, What have I to do with the sacredness of traditions, if I live wholly from within? my friend suggested,—"But these impulses may be from below, not from above." I replied, "They do not seem to me to be such; but if I am the Devil's child, I will live then from the Devil." No law can be sacred to me but that of my nature. Good and bad are but names very readily transferable to that or this; the only right is what is after my constitution, the only wrong what is against it. A man is to carry himself in the presence of all opposition, as if every thing were titular and ephemeral but he. I am ashamed to think how easily we capitulate to badges and names, to large societies and dead institutions. Every decent and well-spoken individual affects and sways me more than is right. I ought to go upright and vital, and speak the rude truth in all ways. If malice and vanity wear the coat of philanthropy, shall that pass? If an angry bigot assumes this bountiful cause of Abolition, and comes to me with his last news from Barbadoes, why should I not say to him, "Go love thy infant; love thy wood-chopper: be good-natured and modest: have that grace; and never varnish your hard, uncharitable ambition with this incredible tenderness for black folk a thousand miles off. Thy love afar is spite at home." Rough and graceless would be such greeting, but truth is handsomer than the affectation of love. Your goodness must have some edge to it,—else it is none. The doctrine of hatred must be preached as the counteraction of the doctrine of love when that pules and whines. I shun father and mother and wife and brother, when my genius calls me. I would write on the lintels of the door-post, *Whim*. I hope it is somewhat better than whim

Perception is how we reclaim resilience, and redirect the gaze. It's how we reverse perspective and refocus our work. It's how we reset our own psychological boundaries when the physical ones around us have been so rattled. Shifting perspective is more than a coping mechanism: it's a creative strategy for survival...

"If we live truly," wrote Emerson, "we shall see truly."

On **closure**
70

Nothing
is at last
sacred
but the
integrity
of your
own mind.

YOUR

GOOD

NESS

at last, but we cannot spend the day in explanation. Expect
me not to show cause why I seek or why I exclude company.
Then, again, do not tell me, as a good man did to-day, of
my obligation to put all poor men in good situations.
Are they *my* poor? I tell thee, thou foolish philanthropist,
that I grudge the dollar, the dime, the cent, I give to such
men as do not belong to me and to whom I do not belong.
There is a class of persons to whom by all spiritual affinity
I am bought and sold; for them I will go to prison, if need
be; but your miscellaneous popular charities; the education at college of fools; the building of meeting-houses
to the vain end to which many now stand; alms to sots;
and the thousandfold Relief Societies;—though I confess
with shame I sometimes succumb and give the dollar,
it is a wicked dollar which by and by I shall have the
manhood to withhold.

Virtues are, in the popular estimate, rather the excep-
tion than the rule. There is the man *and* his virtues. Men
do what is called a good action, as some piece of courage

MUST HAVE SOME edge

or charity, much as they would pay a fine in expiation of daily non-appearance on parade. Their works are done as an apology or extenuation of their living in the world,—as invalids and the insane pay a high board. Their virtues are penances. I do not wish to expiate, but to live. My life is for itself and not for a spectacle. I much prefer that it should be of a lower strain, so it be genuine and equal, than that it should be glittering and unsteady. I wish it to be sound and sweet, and not to need diet and bleeding. I ask primary evidence that you are a man, and refuse this appeal from the man to his actions. I know that for myself it makes no difference whether I do or forbear those actions which are reckoned excellent. I cannot consent to pay for a privilege where I have intrinsic right. Few and mean as my gifts may be, I actually am, and do not need for my own assurance or the assurance of my fellows any secondary testimony.

What I must do is all that concerns me, not what the people think. This rule, equally arduous in actual and in intellectual life, may serve for the whole distinction between greatness and meanness. It is the harder, because you will always find those who think they know what is your duty better than you know it. It is easy in the world to live after the world's opinion; it is easy in solitude to live after our own; but the great man is he who in the midst of the crowd keeps with perfect sweetness the independence of solitude.

The objection to conforming to usages that have become dead to you is, that it scatters your force. It loses your time and blurs the impression of your character. If you maintain a dead church, contribute to a dead Bible-society, vote with a great party either for the government or against it, spread your table like base housekeepers,—under all these screens I have difficulty to detect the precise man you are. And, of course, so much force is withdrawn from your proper life. But do your work, and I shall know you. Do your work, and you shall reinforce yourself. A man must consider what a blindman's-buff is this game of conformity. If I know your sect, I anticipate your argument. I hear a preacher announce for his text and topic the expediency of one of the institutions of his church. Do I not know beforehand that not possibly can he say a new and spontaneous word? Do I not know that, with all this ostentation of examining the grounds of the institution, he will do no such thing? Do I not know that he is pledged to himself not to look but at one side,—the permitted side, not as a man, but as a parish minister? He is a retained attorney, and these airs of the bench are the emptiest affectation. Well, most men have bound their eyes with one or another handkerchief, and attached themselves to some one of these communities of opinion. This conformity makes them not false in a few particulars, authors of a few lies, but false in all particulars. Their every truth is not quite true. Their two is not the real two, their four not the real four; so that every word they say chagrins us, and we know not where to begin to set them right. Meantime nature is not slow to equip us in the prison-uniform of the party to which we adhere. We come to wear one cut of face and figure, and acquire by degrees the gentlest asinine expression. There is a mortifying experience in particular, which does not fail to wreak itself also in the general history; I mean "the foolish face of praise," the forced smile which we put on in company where we do not feel at ease in answer to conversation which does not interest us. The muscles, not spontaneously moved, but moved by a low usurping wilfulness, grow tight about the outline of the face with the most disagreeable sensation.

For nonconformity the world whips you with its displeasure. And therefore a man must know how to estimate a sour face. The by-standers look askance on him in the public street or in the friend's parlour. If this aversation had its origin in contempt and resistance like his own, he might well go home with a sad countenance; but the sour faces of the multitude, like their sweet faces, have no deep cause, but are put on and off as the wind blows and a newspaper directs. Yet is the discontent of the multitude more formidable than that of the senate and the college. It is easy enough for a firm man who knows the world to brook the rage of the cultivated classes. Their rage is decorous and prudent, for they are timid as being very vulnerable themselves. But when to their feminine rage the indignation of the people is added, when the ignorant and the poor are aroused, when the unintelligent brute force that lies at the bottom of society is made to growl and mow, it needs the habit of magnanimity and religion to treat it godlike as a trifle of no concernment.

The other terror that scares us from self-trust is our consistency; a reverence for our past act or word, because the eyes of others have no other data for computing our orbit than our past acts, and we are loath to disappoint them.

But why should you keep your head over your shoulder? Why drag about this corpse of your memory, lest you contradict somewhat you have stated in this or that public place? Suppose you should contradict yourself; what then? It seems to be a rule of wisdom never to rely on your memory alone, scarcely even in acts of pure memory, but to bring the past for judgment into the thousand-eyed present, and live ever in a new day. In your metaphysics you have denied personality to the Deity: yet when the devout motions of the soul come, yield to them heart and life, though they should clothe God with shape and color. Leave your theory, as Joseph his coat in the hand of the harlot, and flee.

A foolish consistency is the hobgoblin of little minds, adored by little statesmen and philosophers and divines. With consistency a great soul has simply nothing to do. He may as well concern himself with his shadow on the wall. Speak what you think now in hard words, and to-morrow speak what to-morrow thinks in hard words again, though it contradict every thing

See the line from a sufficient **distance**, and it straightens itself to the average tendency.

you said to-day.—"Ah, so you shall be sure to be misunderstood."—Is it so bad, then, to be misunderstood? Pythagoras was misunderstood, and Socrates, and Jesus, and Luther, and Copernicus, and Galileo, and Newton, and every pure and wise spirit that ever took flesh. To be great is to be misunderstood.

I suppose no man can violate his nature. All the sallies of his will are rounded in by the law of his being, as the inequalities of Andes and Himmaleh are insignificant in the curve of the sphere. Nor does it matter how you gauge and try him. A character is like an acrostic or Alexandrian stanza;—read it forward, backward, or across, it still spells the same thing. In this pleasing, contrite wood-life which God allows me, let me record day by day my honest thought without prospect or retrospect, and, I cannot doubt, it will be found symmetrical, though I mean it not, and see it not. My book should smell of pines and resound with the hum of insects. The swallow over my window should interweave that thread or straw he carries in his bill into my web also. We pass for what we are. Character teaches above our wills. Men imagine that they communicate their virtue or vice only by overt actions, and do not see that virtue or vice emit a breath every moment.

There will be an agreement in whatever variety of actions, so they be each honest and natural in their hour. For of one will, the actions will be harmonious, however unlike they seem. These varieties are lost sight of at a little distance, at a little height of thought. One tendency unites them all. The voyage of the best ship is a zigzag line of a hundred tacks. See the line from a sufficient distance, and it straightens itself to the average tendency. Your genuine action will explain itself, and will explain your other genuine actions. Your conformity explains nothing. Act singly, and what you have already done singly will justify you now. Greatness appeals to the future. If I can be firm enough to-day to do right, and scorn eyes, I must have done so much right before as to defend me now. Be it how it will, do right now. Always scorn appearances, and you always may. The force of character is cumulative. All the foregone days of virtue work their health into this. What makes the majesty of the heroes of the senate and the field, which so fills the imagination? The consciousness of a train of great days and victories behind. They shed an united light on the advancing actor. He is attended as by a visible escort of

In medieval France, *distance* might refer to anything from dispute and controversy to quarrel and rebellion, the sorts of conditions intensified by spatial expanse, amplified by physical separation. In contemporary usage, it's a competitive, rather than compassionate word: *going the distance* is a euphemism for endurance, while *leaving someone in the distance* is to surpass them.

Maybe distance was always territorial.

On **loneliness**
72

angels. That is it which throws thunder into Chatham's voice, and dignity into Washington's port, and America into Adams's eye. Honor is venerable to us because it is no ephemeris. It is always ancient virtue. We worship it to-day because it is not of to-day. We love it and pay it homage, because it is not a trap for our love and homage, but is self-dependent, self-derived, and therefore of an old immaculate pedigree, even if shown in a young person.

I hope in these days we have heard the last of conformity and consistency. Let the words be gazetted and

I WILL STAND HERE FOR

"The force of character," Emerson wrote, "is cumulative."

The way we respond to the world, through our work, says everything about who we are, individually and as a people. Responses are reactions, and reactions demand attention. Attention is how we express kindness, commitment, love, and, most critically right now, altruism.

On **character**
74

ridiculous henceforward. Instead of the gong for dinner, let us hear a whistle from the Spartan fife. Let us never bow and apologize more. A great man is coming to eat at my house. I do not wish to please him; I wish that he should wish to please me. I will stand here for humanity, and though I would make it kind, I would make it true. Let us affront and reprimand the smooth mediocrity and squalid contentment of the times, and hurl in the face of custom, and trade, and office, the fact which is the upshot of all history, that there is a great responsible Thinker and Actor working wherever a man works; that a true man belongs to no other time or place, but is the centre of things. Where he is, there is nature. He measures you, and all men, and all events. Ordinarily, every body in society reminds us of somewhat else, or of some other person. Character, reality, reminds you of nothing else; it takes place of the whole creation. The man must be so much, that he must make all circumstances indifferent. Every true man is a cause, a country, and an age; requires infinite spaces and numbers and time fully to accomplish his design;—and posterity seem to follow his steps as a train of clients. A man Cæsar is born, and for ages after we have a Roman Empire. Christ is born, and millions of minds so grow and cleave to his genius, that he is confounded with virtue and the possible of man. An institution is the lengthened shadow of one man; as, Monachism, of the Hermit Antony; the Reformation, of Luther; Quakerism, of Fox; Methodism, of Wesley; Abolition, of Clarkson. Scipio, Milton called "the height of Rome"; and all history resolves itself very easily into the biography of a few stout and earnest persons.

hu
man
ity

SELF-RELIANCE ✦ THE INDIVIDUAL

ET A MAN THEN KNOW HIS WORTH, AND KEEP things under his feet. Let him not peep or steal, or skulk up and down with the air of a charity-boy, a bastard, or an interloper, in the world which exists for him. But the man in the street, finding no worth in himself which corresponds to the force which built a tower or sculptured a marble god, feels poor when he looks on these. To him a palace, a statue, or a costly book have an alien and forbidding air, much like a gay equipage, and seem to say like that, "Who are you, Sir?" Yet they all are his, suitors for his notice, petitioners to his faculties that they will come out and take possession. The picture waits for my verdict: it is not to command me, but I am to settle its claims to praise. That popular fable of the sot who was picked up dead drunk in the street, carried to the duke's house, washed and dressed and laid in the duke's bed, and, on his waking, treated with all obsequious ceremony like the duke, and assured that he had been insane, owes its popularity to the fact, that it symbolizes so well the state of man, who is in the world a sort of sot, but now and then wakes up, exercises his reason, and finds himself a true prince.

RALPH WALDO EMERSON

The soul is not diverse from things,

Our reading is mendicant and sycophantic. In history, our imagination plays us false. Kingdom and lordship, power and estate, are a gaudier vocabulary than private John and Edward in a small house and common day's work; but the things of life are the same to both; the sum total of both is the same. Why all this deference to Alfred, and Scanderbeg, and Gustavus? Suppose they were virtuous; did they wear out virtue? As great a stake depends on your private act to-day, as followed their public and renowned steps. When private men shall act with original views, the lustre will be transferred from the actions of kings to those of gentlemen.

The world has been instructed by its kings, who have so magnetized the eyes of nations. It has been taught by this colossal symbol the mutual reverence that is due from man to man. The joyful loyalty with which men have everywhere suffered the king, the noble, or the great

from $\begin{bmatrix} \textit{space} \\ \textit{light} \\ \textit{time} \\ \textit{man} \end{bmatrix}$ but one with them.

proprietor to walk among them by a law of his own, make his own scale of men and things, and reverse theirs, pay for benefits not with money but with honor, and represent the law in his person, was the hieroglyphic by which they obscurely signified their consciousness of their own right and comeliness, the right of every man.

The magnetism which all original action exerts is explained when we inquire the reason of self-trust. Who is the Trustee? What is the aboriginal Self, on which a universal reliance may be grounded? What is the nature and power of that science-baffling star, without parallax, without calculable elements, which shoots a ray of beauty even into trivial and impure actions, if the least mark of independence appear? The inquiry leads us to that source, at once the essence of genius, of virtue, and of life, which we call Spontaneity or Instinct. We denote this primary wisdom as Intuition, whilst all later teachings are tuitions.

My wilful
actions and
acquisitions
are but
roving;—
the idlest
reverie,
the faintest
native
emotion,
command
my curiosity
and respect.

In that deep force, the last fact behind which analysis cannot go, all things find their common origin. For, the sense of being which in calm hours rises, we know not how, in the soul, is not diverse from things, from space, from light, from time, from man, but one with them, and proceeds obviously from the same source whence their life and being also proceed. We first share the life by which things exist, and afterwards see them as appearances in nature, and forget that we have shared their cause. Here is the fountain of action and of thought. Here are the lungs of that inspiration which giveth man wisdom, and which cannot be denied without impiety and atheism. We lie in the lap of immense intelligence, which makes us receivers of its truth and organs of its activity. When we discern justice, when we discern truth, we do nothing of ourselves, but allow a passage to its beams. If we ask whence this comes, if we seek to pry into the soul that causes, all philosophy is at fault. Its presence or its absence is all we can affirm. Every man discriminates between the voluntary acts of his mind, and his involuntary perceptions, and knows that to his involuntary perceptions a perfect faith is due. He may err in the expression of them, but he knows that these things are so, like day and night, not to be disputed. My wilful actions and acquisitions are but roving;—the idlest reverie, the faintest native emotion, command my curiosity and respect. Thoughtless people contradict as readily the statement of perceptions as of opinions, or rather much more readily; for, they do not distinguish between perception and notion. They fancy that I choose to see this or that thing. But perception is not whimsical, but fatal. If I see a trait, my children will see it after me, and in course of time, all mankind,—although it may chance that no one has seen it before me. For my perception of it is as much a fact as the sun.

The relations of the soul to the divine spirit are so pure, that it is profane to seek to interpose helps. It must be that when God speaketh he should communicate, not one thing, but all things; should fill the world with his voice; should scatter forth light, nature, time, souls, from the centre of the present thought; and new date and new create the whole. Whenever a mind is simple, and receives a divine wisdom, old things pass away,—means, teachers, texts, temples fall; it lives now, and absorbs past and future into the present hour. All things are made sacred by relation to it,—one as much as another. All things are dissolved to their centre

Surrender is the art of uncertainty: It's the practice of giving in, not giving up. And while rupture may be a breaking point, it's not a life sentence.

This is where the magic of the optical unconscious meets the mystery of the human imagination.

Consider it your very own creative stimulus package.

On **uncertainty**
76

by their cause, and, in the universal miracle, petty and particular miracles disappear. If, therefore, a man claims to know and speak of God, and carries you backward to the phraseology of some old mouldered nation in another country, in another world, believe him not. Is the acorn better than the oak which is its fulness and completion? Is the parent better than the child into whom he has cast his ripened being? Whence, then, this worship of the past? The centuries are conspirators against the sanity and authority of the soul. Time and space are but physiological colors which the eye makes, but the soul is light; where it is, is day; where it was, is night; and history is an impertinence and an injury, if it be any thing more than a cheerful apologue or parable of my being and becoming.

Man is timid and apologetic; he is no longer upright; he dares not say "I think," "I am," but quotes some saint or sage. He is ashamed before the blade of grass or the blowing rose. These roses under my window make no reference to former roses or to better ones; they are for what they are; they exist with God to-day. There is no time to them. There is simply the rose; it is perfect in every moment of its existence. Before a leaf-bud has burst, its whole life acts; in the full-blown flower there is no more; in the leafless root there is no less. Its nature is satisfied, and it satisfies nature, in all moments alike. But man postpones or remembers; he does not live in the present, but with reverted eye laments the past, or, heedless of the riches that surround him, stands on tiptoe to foresee the future. He cannot be happy and strong until he too lives with nature in the present, above time.

This should be plain enough. Yet see what strong intellects dare not yet hear God himself, unless he speak the phraseology of I know not what David, or Jeremiah, or Paul. We shall not always set so great a price on a few texts, on a few lives. We are like children who repeat by rote the sentences of grandames and tutors, and, as they grow older, of the men of talents and character they chance to see,—painfully recollecting the exact words they spoke; afterwards, when they come into the point of view which those had who uttered these sayings, they understand them, and are willing to let the words go; for, at any time, they can use words as good when occasion comes. If we live truly, we shall see truly. It is as easy for the strong man to be strong, as it is for the weak to be weak. When we have new perception, we shall gladly disburden the memory

That which you are, Emerson wrote, is "the cumulative force of a whole life's cultivation."

Consider the idea that you have put in serious time leading up to this moment. You've been feeding your mind. You've been training your eye. You've been planting the seeds, tilling the soil, and cultivating the land. It is now time for the harvest.

On **magnanimity** **78**

These roses
under my window
make no reference
to former roses
or to better ones;
they are for what
they are...

There is no time
to them. There is
simply **the rose**;
it is perfect in
every moment of
its existence.

it

if we follow the truth,

of its hoarded treasures as old rubbish. When a man lives with God, his voice shall be as sweet as the murmur of the brook and the rustle of the corn.

And now at last the highest truth on this subject remains unsaid; probably cannot be said; for all that we say is the far-off remembering of the intuition. That thought, by what I can now nearest approach to say it, is this. When good is near you, when you have life in yourself, it is not by any known or accustomed way; you shall not discern the foot-prints of any other; you shall not see the face of man; you shall not hear any name;—the way, the thought, the good, shall be wholly strange and new. It shall exclude example and experience. You take the way from man, not to man. All persons that ever existed are its forgotten ministers. Fear and hope are alike beneath it. There is

will

bring us out safe at last.

somewhat low even in hope. In the hour of vision, there is nothing that can be called gratitude, nor properly joy. The soul raised over passion beholds identity and eternal causation, perceives the self-existence of Truth and Right, and calms itself with knowing that all things go well. Vast spaces of nature, the Atlantic Ocean, the South Sea,—long intervals of time, years, centuries,—are of no account. This which I think and feel underlay every former state of life and circumstances, as it does underlie my present, and what is called life, and what is called death.

Life only avails, not the having lived. Power ceases in the instant of repose; it resides in the moment of transition from a past to a new state, in the shooting of the gulf, in the darting to an aim. This one fact the world hates, that the soul *becomes*; for that for ever degrades the past, turns all

RALPH WALDO EMERSON

The
genesis
and
maturation
of
a
planet

ITS POISE AND ORBIT

the
bended
tree
recovering
itself
from
the
strong
wind

riches to poverty, all reputation to a shame, confounds the saint with the rogue, shoves Jesus and Judas equally aside. Why, then, do we prate of self-reliance? Inasmuch as the soul is present, there will be power not confident but agent. To talk of reliance is a poor external way of speaking. Speak rather of that which relies, because it works and is. Who has more obedience than I masters me, though he should not raise his finger. Round him I must revolve by the gravitation of spirits. We fancy it rhetoric, when we speak of eminent virtue. We do not yet see that virtue is Height, and that a man or a company of men, plastic and permeable to principles, by the law of nature must overpower and ride all cities, nations, kings, rich men, poets, who are not.

This is the ultimate fact which we so quickly reach on this, as on every topic, the resolution of all into the ever-blessed ONE. Self-existence is the attribute of the Supreme Cause, and it constitutes the measure of good by the degree in which it enters into all lower forms. All things real are so by so much virtue as they contain. Commerce, husbandry, hunting, whaling, war, eloquence, personal weight, are somewhat, and engage my respect as examples of its presence and impure action. I see the same law working in nature for conservation and growth. Power is in nature the essential measure of right. Nature suffers nothing to remain in her kingdoms which cannot help itself. The genesis and maturation of a planet, its poise and orbit, the bended tree recovering itself from the strong wind, the vital resources of every animal and vegetable, are demonstrations of the self-sufficing, and therefore self-relying soul.

Thus all concentrates: let us not rove; let us sit at home with the cause. Let us stun and astonish the intruding rabble of men and books and institutions, by a simple declaration of the divine fact. Bid the invaders take the shoes from off their feet, for God is here within. Let our simplicity judge them, and our docility to our own law demonstrate the poverty of nature and fortune beside our native riches.

But now we are a mob. Man does not stand in awe of man, nor is his genius admonished to stay at home, to put itself in communication with the internal ocean, but it goes abroad to beg a cup of water of the urns of other men. We must go alone. I like the silent church before the service begins, better than any preaching. How far off, how cool, how chaste the persons look, begirt each one with a precinct or sanctuary! So let us always sit. Why should we

Discerning is a practice, a process, but it is also a virtue. It requires focus and wonder, humility and bravery, a firm embrace of the universal with the unique. It takes work to see what is not yet in focus, to be who you truly are. Approach your practice with an open mind and a generous heart. Remember that losing yourself in your work means finding yourself in it, too. And delight in the idea that sometimes, as the poet Jack Gilbert so beautifully wrote, "We must unlearn the constellations to see the stars."

On **love**
80

WE MUST GO

assume the faults of our friend, or wife, or father, or child, because they sit around our hearth, or are said to have the same blood? All men have my blood, and I have all men's. Not for that will I adopt their petulance or folly, even to the extent of being ashamed of it. But your isolation must not be mechanical, but spiritual, that is, must be elevation. At times the whole world seems to be in conspiracy to importune you with emphatic trifles. Friend, client, child, sickness, fear, want, charity, all knock at once at thy closet door, and say,—"Come out unto us." But keep thy state; come not into their confusion. The power men possess to annoy me, I give them by a weak curiosity. No man can come near me but through my act. "What we love that we have, but by desire we bereave ourselves of the love."

ALONE.

If we cannot at once rise to the sanctities of obedience and faith, let us at least resist our temptations; let us enter into the state of war, and wake Thor and Woden, courage and constancy, in our Saxon breasts. This is to be done in our smooth times by speaking the truth. Check this lying hospitality and lying affection. Live no longer to the expectation of these deceived and deceiving people with whom we converse. Say to them, O father, O mother, O wife, O brother, O friend, I have lived with you after appearances hitherto. Henceforward I am the truth's. Be it known unto you that henceforward I obey no law less than the eternal law. I will have no covenants but proximities. I shall endeavour to nourish my parents, to support my family, to be the chaste husband of one wife,—but these relations I must fill after a new and unprecedented way. I appeal from your customs. I must be myself. I cannot break myself any longer for you, or you. If you can love me for what I am, we shall be the happier. If you cannot, I will still seek to deserve that you should. I will not hide my tastes or aversions. I will so trust that what is deep is holy, that I will do strongly before the sun and moon whatever inly rejoices me, and the heart appoints. If you are noble, I will love you; if you are not, I will not hurt you and myself by hypocritical attentions. If you are true, but not in the same truth with me, cleave to your companions; I will seek my own. I do this not selfishly, but humbly and truly. It is alike your interest, and mine, and all men's, however long we have dwelt in lies, to live in truth. Does this sound harsh to-day? You will soon love what is dictated by your nature as well as mine, and, if we follow the truth, it will bring us out safe at last.—But so you may give these friends pain. Yes, but I cannot sell my liberty and my power, to save their sensibility. Besides, all persons have their moments of reason, when they look out into the region of absolute truth; then will they justify me, and do the same thing.

The populace think that your rejection of popular standards is a rejection of all standard, and mere antinomianism; and the bold sensualist will use the name of philosophy to gild his crimes. But the law of consciousness abides. There are two confessionals, in one or the other of which we must be shriven. You may fulfil your round of duties by clearing yourself in the *direct*, or in the *reflex* way. Consider whether you have satisfied your relations to father, mother, cousin, neighbour, town, cat, and dog; whether any of these can upbraid you. But I may also neglect this reflex standard, and absolve me to myself. I have my own stern claims and perfect circle. It denies the name of duty to many offices that are called duties. But if I can discharge its debts, it enables me to dispense with the popular code. If any one imagines that this law is lax, let him keep its commandment one day.

And truly it demands something godlike in him who has cast off the common motives of humanity, and has ventured to trust himself for a taskmaster. High be his heart, faithful his will, clear his sight, that he may in good earnest be doctrine, society, law, to himself, that a simple purpose may be to him as strong as iron necessity is to others!

Emerson's true daring lay in his willingness to remain intellectually agnostic, drawing from multiple sources and working both across and between disciplines. He thought about cognition and perception, considered reason and intuition, and believed in history as a rich, vital form of biography.

Most importantly, he resisted doing things the same way twice. He championed getting out of your own way, taking chances, making discoveries, and trusting your gut.

On **alchemy**
82

If you are noble,
I will love you;
if you are not,
I will not hurt you
and myself by
hypocritical
attentions.

SELF-RELIANCE ✚ SOCIETY

F ANY MAN CONSIDER THE PRESENT ASPECTS
of what is called by distinction *society*, he will see the
need of these ethics. The sinew and heart of man seem
to be drawn out, and we are become timorous, despond-
ing whimperers. We are afraid of truth, afraid of fortune,
afraid of death, and afraid of each other. Our age yields
no great and perfect persons. We want men and women
who shall renovate life and our social state, but we see
that most natures are insolvent, cannot satisfy their own
wants, have an ambition out of all proportion to their
practical force, and do lean and beg day and night con-
tinually. Our housekeeping is mendicant, our arts, our
occupations, our marriages, our religion, we have not
chosen, but society has chosen for us. We are parlour
soldiers. We shun the rugged battle of fate, where strength
is born.

If our young men miscarry in their first enterprises,
they lose all heart. If the young merchant fails, men say
he is *ruined*. If the finest genius studies at one of our
colleges, and is not installed in an office within one
year afterwards in the cities or suburbs of Boston or
New York, it seems to his friends and to himself that
he is right in being disheartened, and in complaining

the rest of his life. A sturdy lad from New Hampshire or Vermont, who in turn tries all the professions, who teams it, farms it, peddles, keeps a school, preaches, edits a newspaper, goes to Congress, buys a township, and so forth, in successive years, and always, like a cat, falls on his feet, is worth a hundred of these city dolls. He walks abreast with his days, and feels no shame in not "studying a profession," for he does not postpone his life, but lives already. He has not one chance, but a hundred chances. Let a Stoic open the resources of man, and tell men they are not leaning willows, but can and must detach themselves; that with the exercise of self-trust, new powers shall appear; that a man is the word made flesh, born to shed healing to the nations, that he should be ashamed of our compassion, and that the moment he acts from himself, tossing the laws, the books, idolatries, and customs out of the window, we pity him no more, but thank and revere him,—and that teacher shall restore the life of man to splendor, and make his name dear to all history.

It is easy to see that a greater self-reliance must work a revolution in all the offices and relations of men; in their religion; in their education; in their pursuits; their modes of living; their association; in their property; in their speculative views.

There are many ways to stay sharp in the studio, some seemingly counterintuitive because they involve locating sources of creative nourishment that might not appear obvious. You need sustenance, but you also need serendipity: routes you can revisit, but also routines you can break.

And as paradoxical as it may seem, narrowing your gaze to focus on perfectionism might not be the most direct path to maintaining your edge.

On **chance**
84

01

IN WHAT PRAYERS DO MEN ALLOW THEMSELVES! That which they call a holy office is not so much as brave and manly. Prayer looks abroad and asks for some foreign addition to come through some foreign virtue, and loses itself in endless mazes of natural and supernatural, and mediatorial and miraculous. Prayer that craves a particular commodity,—any thing less than all good,—is vicious. Prayer is the contemplation of the facts of life from the highest point of view. It is the soliloquy of a beholding and jubilant soul. It is the spirit of God pronouncing his works good. But prayer as a means to effect a private end is meanness and theft. It supposes dualism and not unity in nature and consciousness. As soon as the man is at one with God, he will not beg. He will then see prayer in all action. The prayer of the farmer kneeling in his field to weed it, the prayer of the rower kneeling with

He
has
not
one

chance

but
a
hundred
chances.

the stroke of his oar, are true prayers heard throughout nature, though for cheap ends. Caratach, in Fletcher's Bonduca, when admonished to inquire the mind of the god Audate, replies,—

His hidden meaning lies in our endeavours;
Our valors are our best gods.

Another sort of false prayers are our regrets. Discontent is the want of self-reliance: it is infirmity of will. Regret calamities, if you can thereby help the sufferer; if not, attend your own work, and already the evil begins to be repaired. Our sympathy is just as base. We come to them who weep foolishly, and sit down and cry for company, instead of imparting to them truth and health in rough electric shocks, putting them once more in communication with their own reason. The secret of fortune is joy in our hands. Welcome evermore to gods and men is the self-helping man. For him all doors are flung wide: him all tongues greet, all honors crown, all eyes follow with desire. Our love goes out to him and embraces him, because he did not need it. We solicitously and apologetically caress and celebrate him, because he held on his way and scorned our disapprobation. The gods love him because men hated him. "To the persevering mortal," said Zoroaster, "the blessed Immortals are swift."

As men's prayers are a disease of the will, so are their creeds a disease of the intellect. They say with those foolish Israelites, "Let not God speak to us, lest we die. Speak thou, speak any man with us, and we will obey." Everywhere I am hindered of meeting God in my brother, because he has shut his own temple doors, and recites fables merely of his brother's, or his brother's brother's God. Every new mind is a new classification. If it prove a mind of uncommon activity and power, a Locke, a Lavoisier, a Hutton, a Bentham, a Fourier, it imposes its classification on other men, and lo! a new system. In proportion to the depth of the thought, and so to the number of the objects it touches and brings within reach of the pupil, is his complacency. But chiefly is this apparent in creeds and churches, which are also classifications of some powerful mind acting

on the elemental thought of duty, and man's relation to the Highest. Such is Calvinism, Quakerism,
Swedenborgism. The pupil takes the same delight in
subordinating every thing to the new terminology, as
a girl who has just learned botany in seeing a new
earth and new seasons thereby. It will happen for a
time, that the pupil will find his intellectual power
has grown by the study of his master's mind. But in
all unbalanced minds, the classification is idolized,
passes for the end, and not for a speedily exhaustible
means, so that the walls of the system blend to their
eye in the remote horizon with the walls of the universe; the luminaries of heaven seem to them hung on
the arch their master built. They cannot imagine how
you aliens have any right to see,—how you can see;
"It must be somehow that you stole the light from us."
They do not yet perceive, that light, unsystematic,
indomitable, will break into any cabin, even into theirs.
Let them chirp awhile and call it their own. If they are
honest and do well, presently their neat new pinfold
will be too strait and low, will crack, will lean, will
rot and vanish, and the immortal light, all young and
joyful, million-orbed, million-colored, will beam over
the universe as on the first morning.

O2

IT IS FOR WANT OF SELF-CULTURE THAT THE
superstition of Travelling, whose idols are Italy, England,
Egypt, retains its fascination for all educated Americans.
They who made England, Italy, or Greece venerable in
the imagination did so by sticking fast where they were,
like an axis of the earth. In manly hours, we feel that duty
is our place. The soul is no traveller; the wise man stays
at home, and when his necessities, his duties, on any
occasion call him from his house, or into foreign lands,
he is at home still, and shall make men sensible by the
expression of his countenance, that he goes the mission-
ary of wisdom and virtue, and visits cities and men like a
sovereign, and not like an interloper or a valet.

I have no churlish objection to the circumnaviga-
tion of the globe, for the purposes of art, of study, and
benevolence, so that the man is first domesticated, or
does not go abroad with the hope of finding somewhat

greater than he knows. He who travels to be amused, or to get somewhat which he does not carry, travels away from himself, and grows old even in youth among old things. In Thebes, in Palmyra, his will and mind have become old and dilapidated as they. He carries ruins to ruins.

Travelling is a fool's paradise. Our first journeys discover to us the indifference of places. At home I dream that at Naples, at Rome, I can be intoxicated with beauty, and lose my sadness. I pack my trunk, embrace my friends, embark on the sea, and at last wake up in Naples, and there beside me is the stern fact, the sad self, unrelenting, identical, that I fled from. I seek the Vatican, and the palaces. I affect to be intoxicated with sights and suggestions, but I am not intoxicated. My giant goes with me wherever I go.

03

BUT THE RAGE OF TRAVELLING IS A SYMPTOM of a deeper unsoundness affecting the whole intellectual action. The intellect is vagabond, and our system of education fosters restlessness. Our minds travel when our bodies are forced to stay at home. We imitate; and what is imitation but the travelling of the mind? Our houses are built with foreign taste; our shelves are garnished with foreign ornaments; our opinions, our tastes, our faculties, lean, and follow the Past and the Distant. The soul created the arts wherever they have flourished. It was in his own mind that the artist sought his model. It was an application of his own thought to the thing to be done and the conditions to be observed. And why need we copy the Doric or the Gothic model? Beauty, convenience, grandeur of thought, and quaint expression are as near to us as to any, and if the American artist will study with hope and love the precise thing to be done by him, considering the climate, the soil, the length of the day, the wants of the people, the habit and form of the government, he will create a house in which all these will find themselves fitted, and taste and sentiment will be satisfied also.

Insist on yourself; never imitate. Your own gift you can present every moment with the cumulative force

Admission is a kind of permission that follows the pursuit and path of external validation: it's demonstrative, quantifiable, and visible, a form of *granting access*. (An attorney is *admitted* to the bar. Tickets *admit* you to a performance.) But invert the model and now that validation is internalized: it's emotional, remote, and invisible, a form of *giving in*.

It is far easier to externalize than to admit. Easier to work than to want.

On **authenticity**
86

what is
imitation

but

the
travelling

of

the
mind?

obey

of a whole life's cultivation; but of the adopted talent of another, you have only an extemporaneous, half possession. That which each can do best, none but his Maker can teach him. No man yet knows what it is, nor can, till that person has exhibited it. Where is the master who could have taught Shakspeare? Where is the master who could have instructed Franklin, or Washington, or Bacon, or Newton? Every great man is a unique. The Scipionism of Scipio is precisely that part he could not borrow. Shakspeare will never be made by the study of Shakspeare. Do that which is assigned you, and you cannot hope too much or dare too much. There is at this moment for you an utterance brave and grand as that of the colossal chisel of Phidias, or trowel of the Egyptians, or the pen of Moses, or Dante, but different from all these. Not possibly will the soul all rich, all eloquent, with thousand-cloven tongue, deign to repeat itself; but if you can hear what these patriarchs say, surely you can reply to them in the same pitch of voice; for the ear and the tongue are two organs of one nature. Abide in the simple and noble regions of thy life, obey thy heart, and thou shalt reproduce the Foreworld again.

thy heart

04

AS OUR RELIGION, OUR EDUCATION, OUR ART look abroad, so does our spirit of society. All men plume themselves on the improvement of society, and no man improves.

Society never advances. It recedes as fast on one side as it gains on the other. It undergoes continual changes; it is barbarous, it is civilized, it is christianized, it is rich, it is scientific; but this change is not amelioration. For every thing that is given, something is taken. Society acquires new arts, and loses old instincts. What a contrast between the well-clad, reading, writing, thinking American, with a watch, a pencil, and a bill of exchange in his pocket, and the naked New Zealander, whose property is a club, a spear, a mat, and an undivided twentieth of a shed to sleep under! But compare the health of the two men, and you shall see that the white man has lost his aboriginal strength. If the traveller tell us truly, strike the savage with a broad axe, and in a day or two the flesh shall unite and heal as if you struck the blow into soft pitch, and the same blow shall send the white to his grave.

The civilized man has built a coach, but has lost the use of his feet. He is supported on crutches, but

The heart wants what it wants.

Emily Dickinson wrote those consoling words to a friend whose husband was about to leave on an extended voyage. "Not to see what we love," she wrote, "is very terrible."

Dickinson wasn't wrong. Wanting what is not possible—no matter how you define your object of desire—is a recipe for disappointment.

On **Individualism 88**

lacks so much support of muscle. He has a fine Geneva watch, but he fails of the skill to tell the hour by the sun. A Greenwich nautical almanac he has, and so being sure of the information when he wants it, the man in the street does not know a star in the sky. The solstice he does not observe; the equinox he knows as little; and the whole bright calendar of the year is without a dial in his mind. His note-books impair his memory; his libraries overload his wit; the insurance-office increases the number of accidents; and it may be a question whether machinery does not encumber; whether we have not lost by refinement some energy, by a Christianity entrenched in establishments and forms, some vigor of wild virtue. For every Stoic was a Stoic; but in Christendom where is the Christian?

There is no more deviation in the moral standard than in the standard of height or bulk. No greater men are now than ever were. A singular equality may be observed between the great men of the first and of the last ages; nor can all the science, art, religion, and philosophy of the nineteenth century avail to educate greater men than Plutarch's heroes, three or four and twenty centuries ago. Not in time is the race progressive. Phocion, Socrates, Anaxagoras, Diogenes, are great men, but they leave no class. He who is really of their class will not be called by their name, but will be his own man, and, in his turn, the founder of a sect. The arts and inventions of each period are only its costume, and do not invigorate men. The harm of the improved machinery may compensate its good. Hudson and Behring accomplished so much in their fishing-boats, as to astonish Parry and Franklin, whose equipment exhausted the resources of science and art. Galileo, with an opera-glass, discovered a more splendid series of celestial phenomena than any one since. Columbus found the New World in an undecked boat. It is curious to see the periodical disuse and perishing of means and machinery, which were introduced with loud laudation a few years or centuries before. The great genius returns to essential man. We reckoned the improvements of the art of war among the triumphs of science, and yet Napoleon conquered Europe by the bivouac, which consisted of falling back on naked valor, and disencumbering it of all aids. The Emperor held it impossible to make a perfect army, says Las Casas, "without abolishing our arms, magazines, commissaries, and carriages, until, in imitation of the Roman custom, the soldier should receive his supply of corn, grind it in his hand-mill, and bake his bread himself."

Society is a wave. The wave moves onward, but the water of which it is composed does not. The same particle does not rise from the valley to the ridge. Its unity is only phenomenal. The persons who make up a nation to-day, next year die, and their experience with them.

And so the reliance on Property, including the reliance on governments which protect it, is the want of self-reliance. Men have looked away from themselves and at things so long, that they have come to esteem the religious, learned, and civil institutions as guards of property, and they deprecate assaults on these, because they feel them to be assaults on property. They measure their esteem of each other by what each has, and not by what each is. But a cultivated man becomes ashamed of his property, out of new respect for his nature. Especially he hates what he has, if he see that it is accidental,—came to him by inheritance, or gift, or crime; then he feels that it is not having; it does not belong to him, has no root in him, and merely lies there, because no revolution or no robber takes it away. But that which a man is does always by necessity acquire, and what the man acquires is living property, which does not wait the beck of rulers, or mobs, or revolutions, or fire, or storm, or bankruptcies, but perpetually renews itself wherever the man breathes. "Thy lot or portion of life," said the Caliph Ali, "is seeking after thee; therefore be at rest from seeking after it." Our dependence on these foreign goods leads us to our slavish respect for numbers. The political parties meet in numerous conventions; the greater the concourse, and with each new uproar of announcement, The delegation from Essex! The Democrats from New Hampshire! The Whigs of Maine! the young patriot feels himself stronger than before by a new thousand of eyes and arms. In like manner the reformers summon conventions, and vote and resolve in multitude. Not so, O friends! will the God deign to enter and inhabit you, but by a method precisely the reverse. It is only as a man puts off all foreign support, and stands alone, that I see him to be strong and to prevail. He is weaker by every recruit to his banner. Is not a man better than a town? Ask nothing of men, and in the endless mutation, thou only firm column must

My giant goes with me

presently appear the upholder of all that surrounds thee. He who knows that power is inborn, that he is weak because he has looked for good out of him and elsewhere, and so perceiving, throws himself unhesitatingly on his thought, instantly rights himself, stands in the erect position, commands his limbs, works miracles; just as a man who stands on his feet is stronger than a man who stands on his head.

So use all that is called Fortune. Most men gamble with her, and gain all, and lose all, as her wheel rolls.

We tell ourselves
stories, as Joan
Didion long ago
observed, in order
to live

I go.

But we also tell
ourselves stories
to make sense
of the world.
Our imperfections
laid bare, our
narratives set
free, the mind is
gloriously liberated
when we share
them with the
world. Which we
do. Which we must.

wherever

In what might be
the most perfect
phrase in Ralph
Waldo Emerson's
essay on self-
reliance, he makes
the following,
rather timely
observation:
"Our minds travel
when our bodies
are forced to stay
at home."

On **narrative**
90

But do thou leave as unlawful these winnings, and
deal with Cause and Effect, the chancellors of God. In
the Will work and acquire, and thou hast chained the
wheel of Chance, and shalt sit hereafter out of fear from
her rotations. A political victory, a rise of rents, the recovery of your sick, or the return of your absent friend, or
some other favorable event, raises your spirits, and you
think good days are preparing for you. Do not believe it.
Nothing can bring you peace but yourself. Nothing can
bring you peace but the triumph of principles.

RALPH WALDO EMERSON

Our minds travel when our bodies

are
forced
to
stay
at
home.

On gravity.

When I was young, I wanted to be an actor. I wanted to be an actor because I wanted to try on other personalities, to inhabit other people's lives. If I memorized someone else's sentences, I reasoned, I could discard them at the end of the evening. If I dressed in someone else's clothes, my logic continued, I could channel a personality through my body. You make the character move and, more importantly, it moves you.

And then you move on.

An actor pretends, but is not a puppet. Character comes alive not because of those lines and those clothes but because the actor's own character breathes life into it. Each intersection between actor and character is different. Every night of a performance is different. Yet somewhere in the magical alchemy of all that productivity and performance lies a beautiful solo dance between the stage and the self.

Seamus Heaney once wrote that "the faking of feelings is a sin against the imagination."

When is pretending just another word for faking?

Pretending, when grounded in your own authentic spirit, is nothing more than the art of make-believe. You can—indeed, you should—try on other personalities, experiment with different vocabularies and voices. You just have to remember how to come back to center.

But perhaps it's worth considering what it is you're actually faking here. Style? Substance? Influence? Affluence? Are you pretending to be productive by repeatedly redoing what you already know how to do, under the guise of sustaining consistency in your work? Are you doing just what you're expected to do, what's acceptable, if redundant? Worse—are you seeking inspiration from other people's work, siphoning small parts of it as your own?

That's called aping. Like an ape does. Or a parrot.

To wit: in his 1836 essay on nature, Emerson refers to the pantomime of brutes—and yes, he was referring, in this instance, to animals. But his nod to pantomime illustrates another facet of pretending: the idea of mirroring something, reflexively and without cadence—imitation, if you will, as evisceration.

That's called identity theft. Like a criminal does. Or a copyist.

"Imitation is suicide," Emerson famously wrote. "Insist on yourself; never imitate."

The problem with present-day pretending is that it's all too often driven by status and popularity. Long before the lure of mobile technology would make social media a theater all its own, the psychologist

Erving Goffman wrote about dramaturgical loyalty, which is what happens when you feel obligated to keep up appearances, playing the part you're meant to play, even if it's disingenuous. (The question of loyalty is a curious one. To whom are you loyal if not yourself?) Goffman's thoughts on what he termed "self-presentation theory" made a strong case for the power of defined roles, which begs the question: is it still pretending if you stay in character?

And if you stay in character too long, are you faking it?

In one of the most haunting passages from his theatrical masterpiece about the life of Georges Seurat, the American songwriter Stephen Sondheim had a better idea (and a deeply Emersonian one). "Anything you do," sings Dot, Seurat's muse, "let it come from you." (A Sondheim rhyming scheme is never that simple, and Dot ends with a final speculation: "Then it will be new.")

Maybe this is the big distinction. Faking is passive, an expression of lethargy. Pretending is active, an expression all its own. To resist those sins against the imagination is to see anew, and to see anew, you have to keep moving. Loyalty to that requires no puppetry, and needs no stage. Find—and hold tight to—that center. The pretending, and everything that comes with it, will find itself.

On closure.

Many years ago I was working with my students on an experimental project, adapting an early twentieth-century photo album as an interactive website, when we came upon a picture of a young soldier. He was photographed alone, in uniform, standing in an empty field. Below him, someone had written three words:

Taken in France.

We sat there staring at this image together for some time, searching for a narrative we could all agree upon—but we couldn't find one.

"The photograph was taken in France," said one student.

"No, the soldier was taken prisoner in France," said another. "He was actually missing in action."

"No again," said a third. "He was killed in France, and taken from his family."

Three students, three readings, three fully different, yet entirely reasonable explanations.

And a reminder that we never really know what's going on.

The basic state of not knowing is compounded in times of crisis, when our lives are so deeply disrupted. Roles suspended, routines upended, we're shellshocked by the stress of having to put new systems in place— systems that map, often poorly, to our former behaviors.

Under ordinary conditions, for example, the process of making work in the studio is guided by some kind of discipline: the sculptor works from an armature, the designer builds from a grid—all frameworks that support an ensuing exploration. Eliminate that central mechanism, and you're in operational free-fall, untethered to reality. Something is missing.

And when that something is hard to pin down, everything is missing.

This cycle of perpetual disorientation is not unlike something psychologists call ambiguous loss. Caught between presence and absence, you're contending with an emptiness that you can't quite identify, with questions you can't name, with answers you can't possibly find. You feel confused, ashamed, even stigmatized by what you can't understand, let alone control, and because whatever it is you are grieving has no definition, you feel lost.

What's particularly difficult here is that the grief attending such loss is kicked into sensory overdrive not just because you can't find clarity, but because you can't find closure. You miss what you can't have—and you know it—which makes you miss it even more.

Sound familiar?

The term "ambiguous loss" was first used in the 1970s by Pauline Boss, a psychologist who studied the families of soldiers during the Vietnam War (soldiers who were, in fact, missing in action). In the many years since,

she's looked broadly at what happens when roles, situations, expectations, and boundaries are uncertain. She's studied both the paradigms and paradoxes that we cling to, the definitions we demand, and how our dependency on all of them restricts our capacity to thrive.

What's most resoundingly clear in her work, and what's so critical for this moment, is the degree to which closure—the definition we crave most of all—is a myth.

Perception, however, is not. It's how we reclaim resilience, and redirect the gaze. It's how we reverse perspective and refocus our work. It's how we reset our own psychological boundaries when the physical ones around us have been so rattled. Shifting perspective is more than a coping mechanism: it's a creative strategy for survival, one that demands many things, not least of which is tuning into your own self-reliance.

"If we live truly," wrote Emerson, "we shall see truly."

Perhaps, in the end, ambiguous loss is the loss we cannot see, just as it lingers in the closure we cannot find. We're all, in a sense, missing in action just now. The missing part feels interminable, inescapable, and undeniably ambiguous. But the action part? That, it seems clear, is up to you.

On **loneliness**.

The word propinquity refers to spatial nearness, to a physical or psychological proximity that both informs and is informed by personal connection. The propinquity effect, for example, is the tendency to form friendships, even romantic relationships, with those in our midst. (Hard to imagine just now, obviously.)

The opposite of propinquity is distance, the uncertain space between things. That word has a fascinating etymology, originating in Latin with *distantia*— a standing apart. (In Italian, *distare* means *to be distant* but also includes in its root form the verb *stare—to be*.) In medieval France, *distance* might refer to anything from dispute and

controversy to quarrel and rebellion, the sorts of conditions intensified by spatial expanse, amplified by physical separation. In contemporary usage, it's a competitive rather than compassionate word: *going the distance* is a euphemism for endurance, while *leaving someone in the distance* is to surpass them.

Maybe distance was always territorial.

But remove the interpersonal dynamic and a different narrative emerges: now it's about the distance between you and your work. Emotional distance promotes objectivity. Physical distance reasserts scale. Distance is now a method, a formal maneuver that conveys perspective, establishes context, anchors perception, and supports truth.

Social distance, however, is not as easily manouvered, and can just as easily distort truth. ("One sees qualities at a distance," wrote Victor Hugo, "and defects at close range.") But is that such a bad thing? Thoreau believed having one's friends at a distance made the earth seem more spacious, while Emerson, in spite of his staunch views on individualism, described friends as the masterpiece of nature, and friendship as too good to be believed. To miss one's friends was to experience the sensation, as he so eloquently put it, "of an infinite remoteness."

Infinite remoteness, indeed. Standing apart, while essential for public health, is not so easy for mental health.

Will social alienation make us a socially alien nation?

It bears saying that technology in general (and social media in particular) served to socially distance us long before quarantine ever did. It led us to alternative ways to gather, united us around shared affinities, and introduced radical new modes of kinship. Sustained not so much by physical proximity as by shared values, we have learned to navigate, in both real and asynchronous time, to connect as we need.

Just not, perhaps, as we want.

Propinquity, in this context, has more to do with functional than physical distance. And who is to say what distance even looks like? Six feet? Six miles? Six thousand miles? Perhaps what sustains us in our infinite remoteness is just this: the understanding that we don't know the difference, and that it doesn't really matter. Distance is not territorial: it's immaterial. We find each other because we can.

On character.

Some years ago, Mark Morocco, an actor, was in a terrible car accident with his wife, Lisa. Because they were both young, otherwise healthy, and lucky—and because they were quickly attended to by skilled emergency physicians and trauma surgeons—they survived.

A year later, Mark left acting behind to return to school to become an ER doctor. When asked why, he explained that the physicians who saved his life were engaged and passionate, the way artists are engaged and passionate—a characterization that testifies to one man's generosity of character, if nothing else.

Artistic responses to disaster have a rich history all their own, from public art projects to public health campaigns to radical expressions of protest, resistance, and dissent. How, and where, and when—and with what frequency and insistence—we respond to adversity says as much about artists as individuals as it does about the communities within which we work.

Communities themselves crystallize in crisis, unified at the nexus of solidarity (which is communal) and suffering (which is not). Coming to terms with a catastrophe is disorienting, which explains the occasional urge to channel your inner location scout: recalling where you were, say, when JFK was shot, when the Challenger exploded, or when the Twin Towers collapsed. But must you relate to a disaster to give it meaning?

A question for another day.

For now, it bears saying that we each respond to crisis in different ways. Some of us retreat. Others mope. Still others live vicariously through influencers (a questionable term if ever there was one) who persist, for whatever reason, as the deities of choice for a certain swath of the population. When Kylie Jenner posted recently on Instagram, reporting that she was bored, she received more than one hundred thousand comments, and nearly six million likes.

Six. Million. Likes.

For context, that's about two percent of the entire US population. It's the entire population of Denmark. It's the approximate number of Jews who died during the Holocaust.

Don't be fooled. Social media, disguised as communication, and which traffics in the counterintuitive circuitry of the tautological, is not now—nor has it ever been—an art form. It may be tempting to think otherwise, but think of this as a wake-up call.

Witnessing a crisis does not require you to be endlessly productive, but it does offer you the opportunity to shift gears. You can't be passive and passionate at the same time. To be truly self-reliant is to reclaim your own voice, your own mind, your own practice. For now? Stop applauding apathy. Start reclaiming agency. Look hard. Listen harder. Accept that life is unpredictable, that pain is subjective, and that boredom, for God's sake, is not the same as suffering.

Today, Dr. Mark Morocco serves on the front lines as an emergency physician at UCLA. He's a first responder, and has been for nearly three decades. I know of no one more devoted to his patients, his colleagues, and his community—no one, for that matter, more passionate or more engaged, and why?

"The force of character," Emerson wrote, "is cumulative."

The way we respond to the world, through our work, says everything about who we are, individually and as a people. Responses are reactions, and reactions demand attention. Attention is how we express kindness, commitment, love, and, most critically right now, altruism. Generosity of character is everything. The struggle, as it happens, is actually real.

On uncertainty.

Disasters are ruptures between what was and what can no longer be. They rob us of innocence. They rid us of civility. (They remind us of death.) Panic begets panic, the world gets smaller, and the forcefield of the mind goes into vigilant overdrive. We feel vulnerable, disoriented, and lost.

Feeling lost, however, has its benefits. Walter Benjamin, the German essayist and philosopher, believed that to really know a city, you needed to get lost in it. He believed in serendipity and spontaneity, in the power of the optical unconscious, and in the kind

of spirited individualism that Emerson would have applauded. (The almost comically melancholic Benjamin once wrote that solitude was the only fit state of man.) His last work—a robust, unfinished study on the arcades of Paris—was a celebration of the surreal, a liberation from convention, and a prescient commentary on the modern urban condition. The rise of production. The surge of consumerism. Social entropy, visual ambiguity, and cultural dissonance. His arcades were labyrinths of wonder, perceptual loops that generated more loops, like a Piranesi etching or a Pirandello play.

Benjamin's notion of the street connoisseur, or *flâneur* (a notion he attributed to the poet Charles Baudelaire), was a lone figure armed with neither schedule nor map, finding meaning and delight, instead, in their absence. What possible lesson could that teach us now, all of us held hostage in the itinerary-deprived world of extended quarantine? That tourism is not unique to the urban fabric? That wandering is a state of mind? That there might be value in losing yourself? Yes to all.

In her own reading of Benjamin, Rebecca Solnit refers to this kind of loss as "a voluptuous surrender." "Lost in your arms, lost to the world, utterly immersed in what is present so that its surroundings fade away,"

she writes. "To be lost is to be fully present, and to be fully present is to be capable of being in uncertainty and mystery."

Surrender is the art of uncertainty: it's the practice of giving in, not giving up. And while rupture may be a breaking point, it's not a life sentence. This is where the magic of the optical unconscious meets the mystery of the human imagination. Consider it your very own creative stimulus package.

To lose yourself in what Emerson called the "idlest reverie" is to submit to that surrender, to immerse yourself in this ambiguous present, as hauntingly beautiful as those Parisian arcades, just as broken, just as human—and just as surreal.

On magnanimity.

A decade ago, while in residence
at the American Academy in Rome,
I purchased (and, within an hour,
managed to destroy) a very expensive
piece of hand-made paper. I felt totally
inept, and later confessed as much to
the sculptor in the next studio.

"Be gentle with yourself," she replied
reassuringly, "with time and materials."

The lesson? That self-forgiveness is
more productive than self-pity. And
that what you make might matter
less than the acknowledgment of
your own capacity to make it. Those
of us with a hard-won studio practice
know this implicitly, but others may
need a reminder.

So here it is, straight from Ralph Waldo
Emerson.

That which you are, Emerson wrote,
is "the cumulative force of a whole
life's cultivation."

Consider the idea that you have put
in serious time leading up to this
moment. You've been feeding your
mind. You've been training your eye.
You've been planting the seeds, tilling
the soil, and cultivating the land.
It is now time for the harvest.

Harvesting, an agricultural notion,
began as a seasonal conceit (as
in harvesting crops, which are
cultivated to grow, but also—and this

is key—to regrow). To harvest, after all, is to reap what you've sown. Now, consider the design principles of permaculture: regenerative, restorative ecosystems that have as much to do with sustainability practices and habitat integration as they do with diversity, stewardship, and community resilience. Most of all, permaculture is a philosophy of working with (rather than against) that thing called nature. And nature right now obliges us to stay indoors, working in our makeshift studios, and, yes, going it alone.

For anyone brainwashed by the promises of co-creation, trust me: this is good news.

The South African painter and poet Breyten Breytenbach once likened a notebook to a seedbed, making the case for journal keeping as an essential act of self-awareness (harvesting as collecting). Later, the American artist Anne Truitt wrote about the glories of solitude and the idea that time alone allowed for a "sieving of experience" (harvesting as filtering). It's not about the best piece of paper, the fastest connection speeds, or even (or especially) about other people right now, but about focusing on where—but more critically, who—you are.

There's no wrong way to do this, but you'll need to do it on your own. That's the mindset. Studio practice is, fundamentally, a solo endeavor.

Generations of artists at the American Academy in Rome believe that when he was in residence there, the artist Philip Guston struggled with his own studio practice. As the story goes, he is believed to have asked himself this rather beautiful, seminal question: "What kind of work would you make if you thought no one was looking?" he wondered. "Make THAT work."

Which he did.

And so should you.

On love.

You are alone in your studio. You have to find a place to begin whatever it is you are beginning. The metaphor of the ominous blank canvas is everywhere, ready for launch, which can only come from you. There will be input from other sources, not all of it helpful. There will be complexity and confusion, deviations and traps. There will be missteps and accidents, demons and discovery, but none of this will reveal itself unless you dive in, and dive in deep.

You take a breath, and start again. Only this time, you're gentle with yourself, patient with your mind, open to the world—you know what you have to do. The input comes in like the tsunami it is: good cops and bad cops, tossing you here and there. It's work, after all, to make it through to the other side. And the only thing that matters here is that you do.

None of it easy. All of it necessary. And you are the balancing act, navigating it all.

Ralph Waldo Emerson wrote with great compassion about emotional recovery and resilience, about how the bended tree recovers from the strong wind. A humanist by training and a naturalist by choice, he looked for patterns in things, mindfully observing the many ways the world revealed itself, and how that might teach us something about ourselves. As a theorist, he was a chameleon.

Prickly but principled, he could be hyperbolically critical one moment and stunningly compassionate the next. But this was the work at hand: to look at the micro as well as the macro, the uniqueness of the individual against the universality of the human condition.

Somewhere in between lay the act of discernment: part strategy, part sentiment, the work of the self.

Discernment can reveal itself in matters of taste, questions of worth, issues of value, even expressions of hierarchy. It can be moral or psychological, perceptual or liturgical. But mostly it is personal, a solo practice: you discern by yourself, for yourself.

Yet at the opposite end (and there is always an opposite end) this process invites you to consider bigger, more universal ideals, spiritual and immeasurable truths, which may explain why Emerson turned, as he often did, to the poetic. Poetry was rhapsodic, but it was also a form of subterfuge, offering a convenient place to reconcile his unanswerable thoughts. Emerson, being a man of privilege and pride, likely hid behind poetry to say what he himself could not. And here, he was not alone. "Poets," wrote Hannah Arendt, "are the only people to whom love is not only a crucial, but an indispensable experience, which entitles them to mistake it for a universal one."

Because it really is all about love, is it not?

Discerning is a practice, a process, but it is also a virtue. It requires focus and wonder, humility and bravery, a firm embrace of the universal with the unique. It takes work to see what is not yet in focus, to be who you truly are. Approach your practice with an open mind and a generous heart. Remember that losing yourself in your work means finding yourself in it, too. And delight in the idea that sometimes, as the poet Jack Gilbert so beautifully wrote, "We must unlearn the constellations to see the stars." The blank canvas is just the beginning, and beginnings, it must be said, are all about promise. And you have always been ready for that.

On **alchemy**.

The studio is a sanctuary for the imagination. It's where we address discipline and embrace chance. Both are necessary. Neither is optional. The studio is where we learn to wake up to our own motives and to mine our own methods, where we battle with our demons and learn to be brave. Along the way, we try, and we fail. We experiment, and we learn. The studio is the test kitchen: it's where we realize that practice is at once speculative, iterative, and generative.

It's difficult to be generative when life has closed down around you. Difficult, but not impossible.

To generate is to procreate—to beget, like offspring—which calls to mind all sorts of beautiful life cycles, gestational journeys in which ideas take shape, find form, and reveal new sources of light.

Here's one: stop confusing generating with inventing.

To generate an idea is not a foreclosure on an earlier idea. The notion of retracing your steps, revisiting your work, even reworking something you previously produced is no different from, say, grafting rootstock or baking from a sourdough starter. Generative thinking can be restorative sooner than repetitive, expansive rather than reductive. The geometric painter Frederick Hammersley spent entire periods of his prolific career re-making earlier paintings—working something over, painting on the reverse of a canvas, even removing the canvas itself to revisit its tactility, its weave.

All were maneuvers that served to reawaken his thinking and reassert his practice. That new work emanated from such exercises in reconstruction became part of a journey that benefited from time, space, scrutiny — and trust.

But there's something else here, and that's the idea that we generate new work by seeking adjacencies in the liminal spaces bordering the things we already know. There's a kind of implicit alchemy to this idea: the assumption that you are already sitting on a bounty of ideas past. Think of this existing arsenal of thought less as a mysterious abyss than as an abundance of possibility. Take small steps. Venture forth with the strength and presence you've gained from all your hard work up until now.

And then? Go rogue.

In his writing and thinking, Ralph Waldo Emerson's true daring lay in his willingness to remain intellectually agnostic, drawing from multiple sources and working both across and between disciplines. He thought about cognition and perception, considered reason and intuition, and believed in history as a rich, vital form of biography. Most importantly, he resisted doing things the same way twice. He championed getting out of your own way, taking chances, making discoveries, and trusting your gut.

"All life is an experiment," Emerson once wrote. "The more experiments you make the better."

Hammersley, who died in 2009, produced a series of experiments in the 1950s that he later referred to as "hunch" paintings—and what is a hunch but trusting your gut? To answer to intuition is not only deeply Emersonian, but also highly actionable. After all, if the studio is the seed lab, generating is also germinating. Those seeds know exactly what to do.

And so do you.

On chance.

Like most serious artists, the late American painter David Pease went to his studio, without fail, every day of his life. Sometimes he painted. Occasionally, he sketched. Often he revisited his notebooks, or looked through his collections (there were many collections), and sometimes he rearranged the pictures on his wall. On other days, he'd just sharpen his pencils.

The studio was critical. The collections were essential. And the sharpening was a metaphor for everything.

Sharpening a pencil is like fine-tuning an instrument. It's the prep work, like soaking your rice before cooking, or stretching your limbs before running. But as an isolated activity, it has got its

own powerful syntax. It's the art of paying attention.

Sharpening is also a synonym for honing, which is where the process of inspection meets the practice of introspection. (An artist hones a craft. A craftsperson hones a skill.) Honing is polishing and perfecting, but in Old English, it was actually another word for stone: solid and impenetrable, and strong enough to serve as a tool for sharpening something else.

The key phrase here is *something else*.

There are many ways to stay sharp in the studio, some seemingly counterintuitive because they involve locating sources of creative nourishment that might not appear obvious. You need sustenance, but you also need serendipity: routes you can revisit, but also routines you can break.

And as paradoxical as it may seem, narrowing your gaze to focus on perfectionism might not be the most direct path to maintaining your edge.

For David Pease, the nourishment came in those collections: salesman samples, color charts, Froebel blocks, dexterity puzzles, game boards with magnificent grids, and anything to do with the 1939 New York World's Fair—largely because of the Trylon and Perisphere, and yes, he had a collection of those, too. There were marcasite boxes and Krazy Kat cartoons and approximately fifty-four categories of postcards, but the taxonomies were always subject to change, because it was in loosening the grip between definitions that the real work began, leading to new connections, new discoveries, new ideas about everything.

It was not the acquisition of artifacts that fueled Pease's practice so much as the ability to investigate their edges. (Another of sharpening's superpowers: keen observation.) He was a great believer in something called the "chance operation," a theory attributable to John Cage

that entered the studio in the form of play. There were dice and spinners, prisms and rolling logs—tools that randomized choices about color, rhythm, interval, sequence, and choice—liberating the mind to think in new ways.

"You become what you think about all day long," wrote Emerson.

And so it is to sharpen—your pencils, to be sure, but also your own independent mind.

Pease was not alone in this. The late Italian architect Carlo Scarpa famously began all his courses in design at the University of Venice by demonstrating the art of pencil sharpening. To Scarpa, this humble act lay at the core of everything: trusting your eye, guiding your hand, learning how to respect and care for the tools that would become your most trusted partners.

If there is a lesson to be learned here, it's that inspiration is an archaeological dig waiting to happen, but you have to be the one willing to do the digging. This is the work. Now is the time. That sharp ideological spade is as critical to your practice as a sharp pencil ever was, or ever will be. Trusted partners, both. And nothing random about either.

On authenticity.

A decade ago, I bought a house that desperately needed repair. Designed without an architect some thirty years earlier, it had significant defects. That it had exquisite bones seemed meaningless, especially since it wasn't clear there was even a front door. Friends, including my architects, thought I had lost my mind. It was a total wreck. And I was in love.

It was with that love that I ran, headfirst, into renovation. I was a quick study, gaining fast fluency with roofers and plumbers, arguing with contractors, approving budgets. Managing construction became my daily practice. Sourcing materials became my second language. I even had my own tool belt—a Mother's

Day gift—which I wore with immense pride as I set out, day after day, to transform a grim concrete bunker into a light-filled oasis for a family of four.

Then came an illness, and a terminal diagnosis. Priorities shifted, and life slowed down. Seventeen months later, we were a family of three.

I kept going. I dug my heels in and worked even harder. I was now a single parent on a crusade of reconstruction, vowing to finish what I'd started. Somehow, in my tool-belted determination, I equated completing this project with some kind of magical admission to the next phase of my life—of all our lives. At the same time, I couldn't quite admit to myself that this life-changing event was also a death-changing event. But the work itself gave me focus as a maker, purpose as a parent, direction in my waking hours, and enough nighttime preoccupation to keep the cycle in constant rotation. The house became my crucible, and because I could not admit defeat, I kept on.

Admission is a kind of permission that follows the pursuit and path of external validation: it's demonstrative, quantifiable, and visible, a form of *granting access*. (An attorney is *admitted* to the bar. Tickets *admit* you to a performance.) But invert the model and now that validation is internalized: it's emotional, remote, and invisible, a form of *giving in*. (You admit to yourself that you love someone, or something—a defective house, for instance.) It is far easier to externalize than to admit. Easier to work than to want. "To want and not to have—to want and want—how that wrung the heart, and wrung it again and again!" wrote Virginia Woolf.

Productivity is a tonic for loss—not a replacement for it—and the work of reconstruction is always brutal. Moments of prolonged adversity like that one was (and in other ways, like this one is) mean admitting many things to yourself, including the fact that there are no quick fixes, that there are more questions than answers, and that heart-wringing will definitely be involved.

One more thing: work will probably not set you free. But it can help.

Today, that house is my co-parent, sheltering my young adult children while I am sheltering solo, some three thousand miles away. Its defects have mostly been addressed—at least, the ones you can see—though it has taken quite a bit longer to recognize the internal cracks, the kind that require an entirely different set of tools. (I'm still working on those.) Foundations, I have learned, take little time to pour, but quite a bit of time to set. It is only now, a decade after falling in love with a wreck, that I realize the wreck was actually me. It took work, and patience, and an extraordinary amount of love, but I think that now, just maybe, the house loves me right back.

On individualism.

As a child growing up in Paris, I was envious of classmates whose parents worked for the American embassy because they could shop at the American commissary and buy American food. No matter that this was Paris, city of gastronomic delights, a pâtisserie on every corner. No: I was ten, and I longed for graham crackers.

The heart wants what it wants.

Emily Dickinson wrote those consoling words to a friend whose husband was about to leave on an extended voyage. "Not to see what we love," she wrote, "is very terrible."

Dickinson wasn't wrong. Wanting what is not possible—no matter how you define your object of desire—is a recipe for disappointment. It's also a very real consequence of extended quarantine. Captive during the pandemic and forcibly distanced from all that we know and love, the wanting heart is, arguably, left wanting.

Enter longing: the yearning for what we can't have. Longing fuels our appetites, frames our wishes, feeds our love affairs—and makes us sad. Longing for the things we can't connect to makes us even more sad, and sadness reboots that essential, primordial longing. A vicious cycle—and not a very actionable one.

But now think about studio practice, and imagine, conversely, how limitations in a project brief yield new opportunities for expressing ideas. This is a classic concept in art and design education—a pedagogical variant, if you will, of less is more—and one well worth considering as a model for creative life under lockdown. Can disaster be generative? Can deprivation be redemptive? Can less really be more?

Human beings naturally thirst for companionship and contact. We are, after all, a social species, craving exchange and communion, and resisting, by any means necessary, that which makes us feel cast adrift, disconnected, and lonely. "We hunger for intimacy," writes the American historian Jill Lepore. "We wither without it."

Hunger and withering: that's us. But to focus on what's missing might just be missing the point.

Loneliness is a social epidemic that preceded—and will long outlive—this or frankly any pandemic. Dwell on that if you wish, but this might also be a moment for inventing new ways to live and work alone: not as a forgotten fragment of who you were before, but as a whole, grounded, autonomous, independent, and highly individuated person. Imagine confinement as a catalyst for creativity. What might that look like?

Not to have access to what we want may indeed be very terrible. But where there are possibilities, there is hope. "Desire," Emerson wrote, "is possibility seeking expression."

What an exquisite reminder that the mind is flexible, the imagination ever present, and the heart capable of infinite expansion. There are so many ways to see. So many ways to be. And so very many ways to love.

On narrative.

When I was in graduate school, I was obsessed with T.S. Eliot. I read everything he wrote, devoured any biography I could find, and for my thesis exhibition I made an artist's book about him that consisted of a clamshell box filled with found materials, designed to look like they might have been his. The box encapsulated what I loved most about Eliot—his sadness and longing, his dark mind and haunted voice—but even more, it solidified what I loved about making things: the idea that you could immerse yourself in a story, and that if you were successful, other people could immerse themselves in it, too.

There's something about combing through the flotsam of displaced evidence, about locating and recombining material fragments in new ways, something about those magical collisions of history and happenstance that's almost choreographic. You're thinking about space and story; about character and site; about mind and matter; and more than anything else, about time. That last part? Pure Eliot.

The artist's book I made was an early, comparatively primitive attempt to make work that visualized someone's life. And while my Eliot obsession lessened, that essential preoccupation with biography and narrative never left me. Writing. Teaching. Painting. Books. They've all let me experiment with telling stories and, perhaps more importantly, with telling time.

"In my beginning is my end ..." wrote Eliot. "In my end is my beginning." And so it is. Our weeks of shapeless days have taken us across the solstice, from the monotones of winter into the multitudes of spring. These essays, cumulatively, now number more pages than Emerson's original text.

And so, this is a moment to pause— not quite an ending, but not quite a beginning, either. Which may be the entire point.

We seek stories with beginnings and endings, craving the false reassurances of imagined closure. But narratives differ—wildly and ferociously—and we can neither anticipate nor control how they land for others. All of which explains their mystery. And ours.

We tell ourselves stories, as Joan Didion long ago observed, in order to live. But the way we tell them, and the way we digest the stories of others, that's where the work begins: on every page, in every syllable, and in every picture that is, as we all know, worth a thousand words.

But we also tell ourselves stories to make sense of the world. Our imperfections laid bare, our narratives set free, the mind is gloriously liberated when we share them with the world. Which we do. Which we must.

In what might be the most perfect phrase in Ralph Waldo Emerson's essay on self-reliance, he makes the following, rather timely observation: "Our minds travel when our bodies are forced to stay at home."

As we near the end of Captivity 1.0, we know that this was just a practice round. We have learned to be patient, to be still. We have come to tolerate ambiguity, and to embrace loneliness. But we also know that the mind is not as easily restricted, that the imagination cannot so easily be caged. To be truly self-reliant is to trust in that deep well of possibility, of fierce individuality, of honesty—and of hope. In the end, as in the beginning, our stories are just our secrets waiting to be set free.

And for that, we have all the time in the world.

Time and
space are but
physiological
colors which the
eye makes, but
the soul is light...

To talk of
reliance is a
poor external
way of speaking.
Speak rather
of that which
relies, because
it works and is.

All life is an

I must be myself.
I cannot break
myself any
longer for you,
or you. If you
can love me
for what I am,
we shall be the
happier. If you
cannot, I will
still seek to
deserve that
you should.
I will not hide
my tastes or
aversions.

A foolish
consistency is
the hobgoblin
of little minds,
adored by little
statesmen and
philosophers
and divines.

We lie in the
lap of immense
intelligence,
which makes us
receivers of its
truth and organs
of its activity.

Discontent is the want of self-reliance: it is infirmity of will.

When private men shall act with original views, the lustre will be transferred from the actions of kings to those of gentlemen.

experiment.

It is easy in the world to live after the world's opinion; it is easy in solitude to live after our own; but the great man is he who in the midst of the crowd keeps with perfect sweetness the independence of solitude.

Acknowledgments

I am enormously grateful to a number of people who helped make this book possible, beginning with my commissioning editor, Lucas Dietrich (who is credited with having the idea in the first place), and his superb team at Thames & Hudson: Rebecca Pearson, Augusta Pownall, Evie Tarr, and Darren Wall. For their thoughtful contributions to the book's cover, my gratitude to Sir David Adjaye, Lyn Coorg, Maira Kalman, Kensuke Koike, John Maeda, Yuko Shimizu, and Daniella Zalcman.

Our small team at *Design Observer* provided logistical, operational, and no shortage of moral support. Special thanks to Michael Bierut, Blake Eskin, Lee Moreau, Kate Phillips, Will Suzuki, Betsy Vardell, and Hugh Weber. For their participation in our video interviews, thanks to Sara Hendren, De Nichols, Rathna Ramanathan, and Claire Weisz. Thanks, too, to Darren Williams, the musician known as Star Slinger, for putting Emerson's words to music, and graciously permitting us to share his work in our recordings. And to Jarrett Fuller—my favorite design collaborator, a special note of thanks.

Portions of this book were written while I was the Artist in Residence at the California Institute of Technology, where I was made to feel exceptionally welcome. For their many kindnesses, I wish to thank Dehn Gilmore, Catherine Jurca, and Hillary Mushkin. And for inviting me to contribute several of these essays to a special issue of the magazine *Domus*, my thanks to guest editor David Chipperfield.

At Yale, I feel fortunate to have a small number of colleagues who challenge me in all the best ways. Emerson would have loved them, and I do, too: my thanks to Pamela Hovland, Noreen Khawaja, and Joanna Radin. And to my children, Malcolm and Fiona Drenttel, who remind me every day what self-reliance actually looks like: Emerson would have loved you too, but not nearly as much as I do.

All writers require solitude to gestate their ideas, but writing during an extended quarantine presents unique challenges, including, but not limited to, impostor syndrome, paranoia, writer's block, and regular intervals of terror. For their willingness to read early drafts of my essays, an enormous thank you to my Los Angeles friends: Sean Adams, Lawrence Azerrad, Kim Baer, Kevin Bethune, Lorne Buchman, Mark Morocco, Martha Rotman-Snider, Rooh Steif, Chrisann Verges, Lisa Waltz, and Lorraine Wild. And to my friends on the other coast— many of whom were early readers as well—my thanks to Judy Baskin, George Gendron, Melissa Harris, Issa Lampe, Ellen McGirt, Lisa Moose, Maggie Peters, Wendy Richmond, Paula Scher, and Anne Tofflemire.

Emerson famously loathed quotations, but still deserves to have the final word. This book, after all, owes him an enormous debt of gratitude. "Nothing great," he once wrote, "was ever achieved without enthusiasm." He was great. His work was great. We just brought the enthusiasm.

Ralph Waldo Emerson (1803–1882) was an American essayist, lecturer, philosopher, and poet who led the Transcendentalist movement of the mid-nineteenth century. His work, which has held its influence among generations of writers, was remarkable for its originality and independence from popular, consensus-driven beliefs. "In all my lectures," he wrote in his journal in 1840, "I have taught one doctrine, namely, the infinitude of the private man."

Typography

This book was designed by Jessica Helfand and Jarrett Fuller in Emerson and Neue Haas Unica types.

New York printer and book designer Joseph Blumenthal first designed Emerson for his own imprint, Spiral Press, in 1930. Initially known as Spiral (and exclusive to the Press), it was recut by the Monotype Corporation in London, under Stanley Morison's direction, in 1935—the name Emerson deriving from its first appearance in an edition of Ralph Waldo Emerson's essay "Nature." The typeface was digitized by Jerry Kelly and Helen Brandshaft of Nonpareil Type in 2007.

Jessica Helfand's essays are set in Neue Haas Unica, a twenty-first-century hybrid of Helvetica, Univers, and Akzidenz Grotesk, revived in 2015 by designer Toshi Omagari for Monotype.

Page 68
Seamus Heaney.
Preoccupations: Selected Prose 1968–1978.
New York: Faber + Faber, 1980, p. 34

Page 69
Erving Goffman.
The Presentation of Self in Everyday Life.
Garden City, NY: Doubleday, 1959

Page 69
Sunday in the Park with George, 1984.
Music and lyrics by Stephen Sondheim.
Book by James Lapine.

Page 77
Rebecca Solnit.
A Field Guide to Getting Lost. New York: Viking, 2005, p. 13

Page 79
Breyten Breytenbach.
"On Keeping a Notebook." In: *Omnivore: A Journal of Writing and Visual Culture.* New York: The New York Institute for the Humanities at New York University, 2003
+
Anne Truitt.
Daybook: The Journal of an Artist.
New York: Penguin Books, 1984, p. 32

Page 81
Hannah Arendt
The Human Condition.
Chicago: University of Chicago Press, 1958, p. 242, note 81
+
Jack Gilbert.
Tear it Down. In: *The Great Fires: Poems 1982–1992.* New York: Alfred A. Knopf, 2002

Page 87
Virginia Woolf.
To The Lighthouse.
New York: Harcourt Brace and Company, 1927, p. 166

Page 88
Emily Dickinson to Mary Bowles, early summer 1862, in Mabel Loomis Todd (ed.), *The Letters of Emily Dickinson*, vol. 1. Boston: Roberts Brothers, 1894, p. 205

Page 89
Jill Lepore.
"The History of Loneliness."
The New Yorker, March 30, 2020

Page 91
Thomas Stearns Eliot,
Four Quartets. New York: Houghton Mifflin Company, 1943, p. 23

Additional quotes from Emerson are taken from his journals, as well as from the essay "Nature" (1836).

Artist, designer, educator, and a founding
member of *Design Observer*, **Jessica Helfand**
is the author of ten books on visual and cultural
criticism.

Jarrett Fuller is a designer, writer, educator,
editor, and podcaster.

First published in the United Kingdom in 2021
by Thames & Hudson Ltd, 181A High Holborn,
London WC1V 7QX

First published in the United States of America
in 2021 by Thames & Hudson Inc., 500 Fifth
Avenue, New York, New York 10110

Original essay by Ralph Waldo Emerson

Designed by Jessica Helfand + Jarrett Fuller

British Library Cataloguing-in-Publication Data
A catalogue record for this book is available from
the British Library

Library of Congress Control Number
2020951259

ISBN 978-0-500-02447-8

Printed and bound in China by RR Donnelley

Be the first to know about our new releases,
exclusive content and author events by visiting
thamesandhudson.com
thamesandhudsonusa.com
thamesandhudson.com.au